ART OF COLORING

Disney

100

YEARS OF WONDER

100 IMAGES TO INSPIRE CREATIVITY

For Rebecca Cline: You support and empower those around you to think big, dream bold, and follow the paths of creativity and curiosity to new and imaginative heights. By helping to map the farthest plains and deepest seas of Disney history, from Walt's time to today, your work will continue to inspire generations to come.

Editorial Director: **Wendy Lefkon**
Senior Editor: **Jennifer Eastwood**
Senior Designer: **Lindsay Broderick**
Managing Editor: **Monica Vasquez**
Production: **Jerry Gonzalez** and **Marybeth Tregarthen**
Contributing Writers: **Rebecca Cline, Jennifer Eastwood,**
Jim Fanning, Kevin M. Kern, Paula Sigman Lowery
Inker: **John Raymond**

Paperback Edition: ISBN 978-1-368-08370-6
Custom Edition: ISBN 978-1-368-09556-3
FAC-034274-23020

Printed in the United States of America

First Edition, February 2023
1 3 5 7 9 10 8 6 4 2

Visit www.disneybooks.com

ART OF COLORING

Disney

100

YEARS OF WONDER

100 IMAGES TO INSPIRE CREATIVITY

By the Staff of the Walt Disney Archives

Disney
EDITIONS
Los Angeles • New York

ABOVE: Final frame, *Steamboat Willie* (1928).

OPPOSITE AND ON THE FOLLOWING TEN PAGES: Art Deco–inspired art for the Disney100 Celebration.

CONTENTS

PREFACE

ON OCTOBER 16, 1923, A YOUNG MAN FROM the American Midwest signed a contract at his uncle's modest Hollywood home. That contract launched the immediate production of a silent film cartoon series—and a new animation studio. More importantly, it became the foundation of one of the world's most beloved companies—an entertainment powerhouse that has produced incomparable tales of adventure and discovery, magic, music, and the wonders of history and nature all over the globe. It was the beginning of what we know today as The Walt Disney Company.

Walt Disney's passion and vision continue to inspire creativity across the company and for generations of fans. The very concept of what "creativity" is—or what it can be—amounts to a great many things to each of us. Colors. Patterns. Mediums. Each is a tool at the behest of the artist within, ready to help employ perhaps the most precious of humanity's gifts—imagination. When confronted with a blank canvas, sheet of paper, sidewalk, bedroom wall—or any surface, really—one thing unites us in our artistic journey: the decision to adventure forward and make our first mark.

Many of us at the Walt Disney Archives came to work for The Walt Disney Company because its stories, characters, and magical realms have been inspirational sources in each of our own lives. They have helped us make sense of the world around us. And they have driven us to be creative in ways professional and personal.

In honor of the company's first one hundred years, we are thrilled to share a unique look at our history and Walt Disney's legacy, whether it be through *Disney100: The Exhibition* or a variety of commemorative books, including this one. In pulling these coloring pages together, we looked at *thousands* of historical sources, such as vintage press kits, posters, and coloring publications that many of us remember from our own childhoods. We quickly realized that a purely chronological history just would not explain the magic that is "Disney." We felt the best way to approach this book was to share why Walt did what he did. What his own philosophies were and how they inspired him to create such wondrous entertainment.

The line art in this book is organized to support the simple philosophies that Walt shared during his amazing career: the importance of storytelling, the addition of personality to beloved characters, the spirit of adventure and discovery, the wonders of the world around us, the magic in beautiful music, and the excitement of experimentation and innovation. These concepts are what made Walt's creations so very unique and special, and they are still the heart and soul of the stories and experiences that The Walt Disney Company produces today.

We hope this collection inspires you to expand your own creative limits and propels you forward on many artistic adventures. Use pencils, crayons, paint; you name it. Make the following pages *yours*. There's nothing holding you back from covering them with the wildest and most remarkable creations yet as we all celebrate a hundred years of wonder with the company that has been—and will forever be—our favorite wishing star.

—The Staff of the Walt Disney Archives
February 2023

ABOVE: Mickey Mouse • Walt Disney Animation Studios

ABOVE: Minnie Mouse • Walt Disney Animation Studios

ABOVE: Moana • Walt Disney Animation Studios

ABOVE: Tiana • Walt Disney Animation Studios

ABOVE: Snow White • Walt Disney Animation Studios

ABOVE: Simba • Walt Disney Animation Studios

ABOVE: Elsa • Walt Disney Animation Studios

ABOVE: Woody • Pixar Animation Studios

WHERE IT ALL BEGAN

"The way to get started is to quit talking and begin doing."

—Walt Disney[T.1]

The creations of Walt Disney—entrepreneur, innovator, and visionary futurist—would impact the ensuing generations of American popular culture in ways he likely never would have predicted. Several of his key creative philosophies—including the importance of storytelling, creating believable characters, appreciating, and reflecting on the world around us, and constant reinvention—would become touchstones throughout his life's work, generating a creative model that Disney still draws from today. Imagination, invention, inspiration—tenets all that help to understand and describe the drive and growth of Walt's impressive journey from his early life to the establishment of The Walt Disney Company and beyond. From his earliest silent films—including the Alice Comedies and Oswald the Lucky Rabbit shorts—to the origin of Mickey Mouse, Minnie Mouse, and their pals, the elevation and innovation of cartoons as an art form rests not only at the foundation of the entire Disney enterprise, but as benchmarks across an impressive hundred-year journey.

OPPOSITE: Developmental art by Shane Enoch for the gallery poster from *Disney100: The Exhibition*, 2023.

ABOVE AND OPPOSITE: A selection of art from Walt's time in Kansas City, Missouri, including highlights from the pilot film, *Alice's Wonderland* (1923).

OPPOSITE: Alice Comedies movie theater lobby card, c. 1924, featuring Virginia Davis (top), and publicity artwork, c. 1926, showing Walt Disney and Margie Gay (bottom).

ABOVE AND OPPOSITE: Oswald the Lucky Rabbit character poses, 2022.

ABOVE: Minnie Mouse character poses, 2022.

OPPOSITE: *Steamboat Willie*–inspired design illustration, 2022.

ABOVE: Illustration from the first Disney book, *Mickey Mouse Book*, 1930, published by Bibo-Lang.

OPPOSITE: Walt Disney—with a shadow of Mickey Mouse—at his Woking Way home in Los Angeles, c. 1932. Art inked from a photograph by Tom Collins.

WHERE DO THE STORIES COME FROM?

"Sheer animated fantasy is still my first and deepest production impulse. The fable is the best storytelling device ever conceived, and the screen is its best medium."

—Walt Disney[T.2]

"Once upon a time . . ."—these magical words have enthralled listeners for centuries, whether sung by traveling bards or said to children at bedtime. Since Walt's time, creative teams at The Walt Disney Company have taken inspiration from tales both imagined and real from around the world to create completely new characters and experiences that forge emotional connections with audiences of almost every age. Building upon an ongoing legacy of advancing the art of storytelling through believable characters and novel visual worlds, artists create lush environments where the stories come to life. Over the decades, the company has explored numerous sources for its storytelling, from myths, fairy tales, fables, and legends to literary classics and even the much-loved graphic literature of today: comic books. There's almost always a new page to turn, setting our course for the next great adventure.

OPPOSITE: Developmental art by Shane Enoch and David Pacheco for the gallery poster from *Disney100: The Exhibition*, 2023.

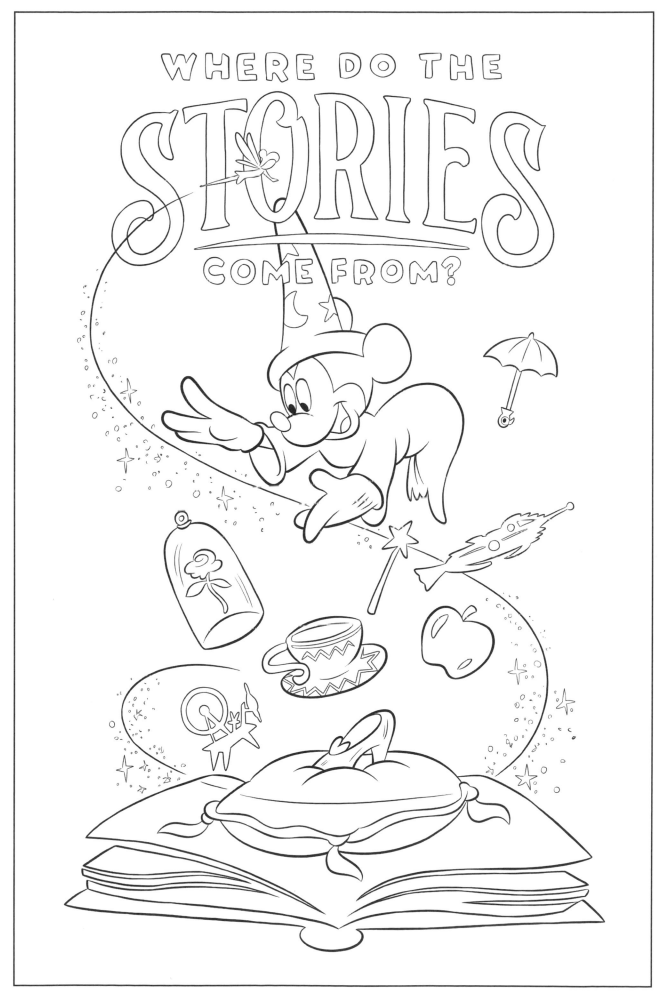

ABOVE: Publicity line art, *The Ugly Duckling*, 1939.

OPPOSITE: Vintage storybook illustration, *Three Little Pigs*, 1933 (inset). *Three Little Pigs* design collage, 2022 (background).

donald duck

ABOVE AND OPPOSITE: Donald Duck character art, 2022 (background). Vintage coloring book line art, *Donald Duck Color Book*, 1936 (insets).

1

2

3

4

5

6

DONALD   DUCK

ABOVE: Story sketch by Albert Hurter from *The Goddess of Spring* (1934, top). Story sketch by a Disney studio artist from *Snow White and the Seven Dwarfs* (1937, bottom) from Walt Disney Animation Studios.

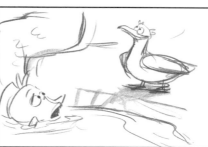

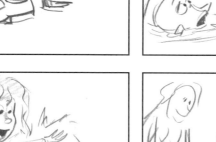

ABOVE: Story sketches by Disney Legend Joe Ranft from *The Little Mermaid* (1989) from Walt Disney Animation Studios.

OPPOSITE: Story sketches by Charles Choo and Madeline Sharafian from *Turning Red* (2022) from Pixar Animation Studios.

ABOVE AND OPPOSITE: Stained glass–like publishing line art inspired by *Beauty and the Beast* (1991) from Walt Disney Animation Studios.

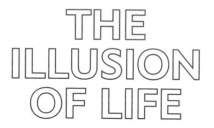

THE ILLUSION OF LIFE

"Animation is different from other parts. Its language is the language of caricature. Our most difficult job was to develop the cartoon's unnatural but seemingly natural anatomy for humans and animals."

—Walt Disney[T.3]

Through all Disney stories and experiences, whether in animation, live-action, or theme park attractions, it is the *characters* who capture our hearts. While a story is a journey, the characters who inhabit that story are what we as the audience care most about. We relate to these characters; we laugh and cry and love with them. They become as real to us as the people in our lives. From their designs by Disney artists to how Disney storytellers explore and develop aspects of their personalities—strengths and weaknesses, hopes and dreams—they are fine-tuned so we the viewers can understand exactly how they think, and why they behave as they do. This magical alchemy is no trick; it's artistry that simulates the very illusion of life.

OPPOSITE: Developmental art by Shane Enoch and David Pacheco for the gallery poster from *Disney100: The Exhibition*, 2023.

How to draw
CHIP and DALE

ABOVE AND OPPOSITE: Vintage publishing line art from *Walt Disney's Tips on Animation* (above; bottom; and opposite, top right and bottom left) and *How to Draw Chip and Dale: A Walt Disney Character Model Guide*, late 1950s.

How to draw PLUTO

PLUTO'S BODY TAPERS

THIN NECK

1/3

ABOVE: Animation drawings by Disney Legend Marc Davis from *Cinderella* (1950) from Walt Disney Animation Studios.

OPPOSITE: Animation drawings by Disney Legend Frank Thomas from *Lady and the Tramp* (1955) from Walt Disney Animation Studios.

ABOVE AND OPPOSITE: Animation drawings by Disney Legend Bill Tytla from *Dumbo* (1941) from Walt Disney Animation Studios.

THE SPIRIT OF ADVENTURE AND DISCOVERY

"We have always tried to be guided by the basic idea that, in the discovery of knowledge, there is great entertainment—as, conversely, in all good entertainment there is always some grain of wisdom, humanity or enlightenment to be gained."

—Walt Disney[T.4]

Spurred by the natural graces of curiosity and wonder, humans have always sought to explore new frontiers, make discoveries, and gain a greater understanding about the world in which we live. Similarly, curiosity, imagination, and risk-taking have long been hallmarks of Disney's exploration of environments and the creation of imaginary yet believable worlds. From the wilds of the jungle to the depths of the oceans, almost every environment offers opportunities to delve deeper and to journey farther, in the name of enlightenment. The drive to learn more about the worlds around us—both real and fictitious—is inherent, and inspiring.

OPPOSITE: Developmental art by Shane Enoch for the gallery poster from *Disney100: The Exhibition*, 2023.

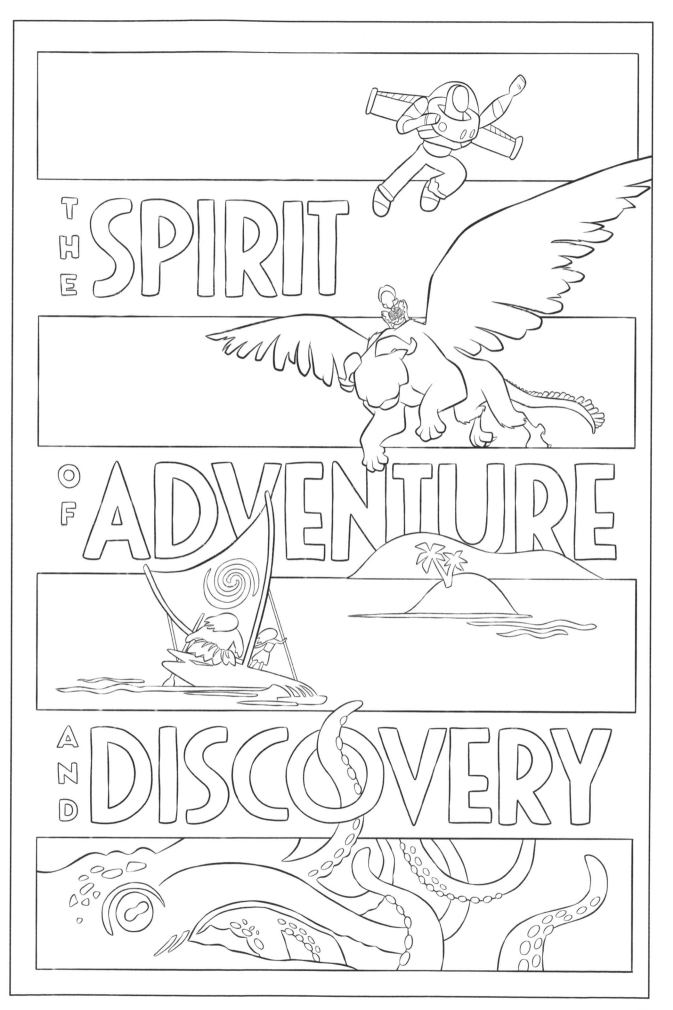

THE SPIRIT OF ADVENTURE AND DISCOVERY

ABOVE: Promotional art for *The Rocketeer* (1991, top) and *Pete's Dragon* (1977, center). Vintage coloring book line art, *Walt Disney Productions presents Bedknobs and Broomsticks Coloring Book*, 1971 (bottom).

OPPOSITE: Memorable moments of favorite characters in flight from Walt Disney Animation Studios (top) and Pixar Animation Studios (bottom).

ABOVE: "Coloring Subject" from Disney studio publicity press book for *Treasure Island* (1950).

OPPOSITE: A collection of cinematic moments from Disney's Pirates of the Caribbean film series.

ABOVE: Coloring contest line art from Disney studio publicity press books for the 1963 theatrical rerelease of *20,000 Leagues Under the Sea* (1954, top) and *The Island at the Top of the World* (1974, bottom).

OPPOSITE: Memorable aquatic adventures highlight the fun to be had above—and below!—the waves.

ABOVE: Coloring contest line art from Disney studio publicity press book for the 1969 theatrical rerelease of *Swiss Family Robinson* (1960, top). Lightcycle publishing line art for *TRON: Legacy* (2010, bottom).

OPPOSITE: Active cinematic adventures abound thanks to some familiar and beloved characters from Walt Disney Animation Studios (top) and Pixar Animation Studios (below).

THE MAGIC OF SOUND AND MUSIC

"Music has always had a prominent part in all our products, from the early cartoon days. So much so, in fact, that I cannot think of the pictorial story without thinking about the complementary music which will fulfill it."

—Walt Disney[T.5]

Sound and music are important aspects of Disney storytelling traditions and are integral to connecting deeply with audiences. While a project's dialogue and characters may speak to our minds, the surrounding soundscape and supporting music speak to our hearts. Walt would push his film songs and scores to be more than catchy tunes. Beginning with *Snow White and the Seven Dwarfs*, he required that music and lyrics help reveal the characters' inner dialogues and move the story forward. Disney songs leap off the screen and into our homes on records, compact discs, and streaming services. They have moved into live theater and onto Broadway stages. They are sung in multiple languages, in our homes, in almost every culture around the globe. For nearly one hundred years, quite simply, Disney music has produced the soundtrack of our lives.

OPPOSITE: Developmental art by Shane Enoch for the gallery poster from *Disney100: The Exhibition*, 2023.

the MAGIC of SOUND and MUSIC

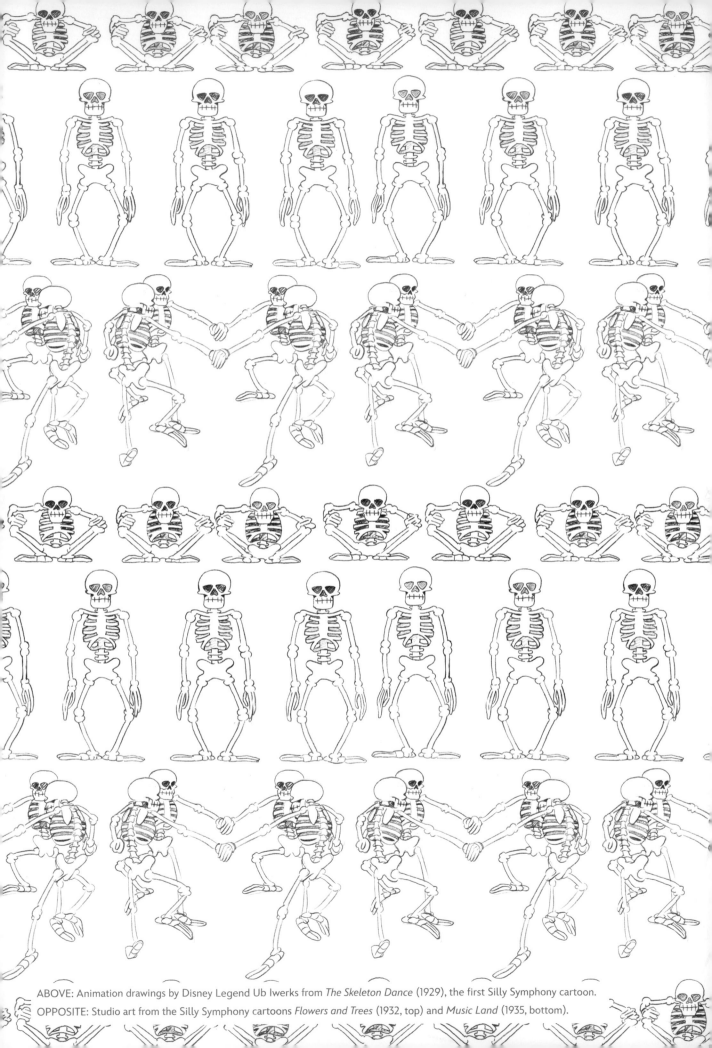

ABOVE: Animation drawings by Disney Legend Ub Iwerks from *The Skeleton Dance* (1929), the first Silly Symphony cartoon.

OPPOSITE: Studio art from the Silly Symphony cartoons *Flowers and Trees* (1932, top) and *Music Land* (1935, bottom).

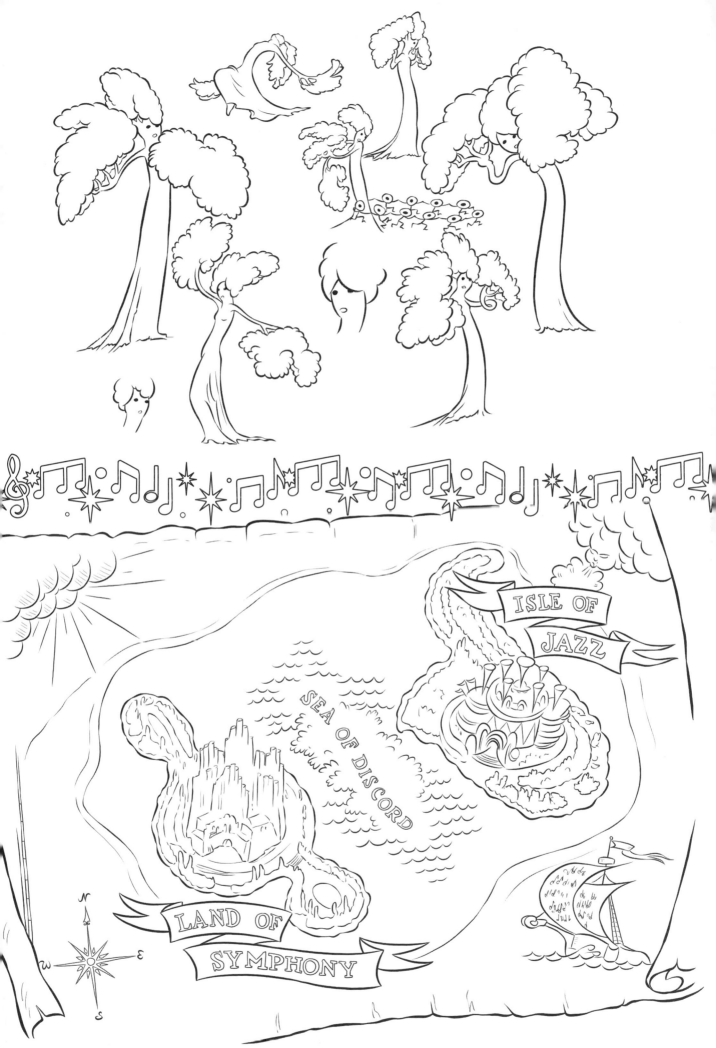

ABOVE AND OPPOSITE: Publishing line art celebrating *Fantasia* (1940, background).
Vintage coloring book line art, *Walt Disney's Fantasia Paint Book*, 1940 (insets).

ABOVE: Coloring contest line art from the Disney studio publicity press book for *Darby O'Gill and the Little People* (1959, top). Line art honoring *Mary Poppins* (1964, bottom) from the Disney Consumer Products Creative Design team.

OPPOSITE: A selection of energetic musical moments from Pixar Animation Studios (top) and Walt Disney Animation Studios (center and bottom), including vintage coloring book line art, *Donald Duck Color Book*, 1936 (center, left).

ABOVE AND OPPOSITE: This selection of line art depicts posters highlighting some of Disney Theatrical Productions' stage shows over the decades.

THE WORLD AROUND US

"The immediate need for education and practice in using our natural resources of soil, forest, water, wildlife and areas of inspirational beauty to the best advantage of all, for this generation and others to come, is again apparent to every observant citizen . . ."

—Walt Disney[T.6]

The beauty and diversity of our planet and its inhabitants are not only sources of storytelling inspiration but represent our global home. Through imagery both real and imagined, Disney has always explored the wonder of a myriad of cultures and customs, reminding everyone that we are all one, and encouraging us to protect and preserve our planet not only for ourselves but for generations to come. From treetop lookouts and deep-sea exploration, to international ports of call and the farthest reaches of space, an adventurous soul will find whole new worlds to embrace with almost every Disney movie, television show, theme park attraction, publication, and beyond. Adventure always beckons across the many realms of Disney history . . . all we have to do is seek it out!

OPPOSITE: Developmental art by Shane Enoch for the gallery poster from *Disney100: The Exhibition*, 2023.

ABOVE: Publishing line art for *Bambi* (1942, background). Promotional Fan Card art, 1975 (top) and vintage coloring book line art, *Walt Disney's Bambi Paint Book*, c. 1941 (bottom).

OPPOSITE: Promotional Fan Card art for *Saludos Amigos* (1943) and product characters poses for *The Three Caballeros* (1945, background).

ABOVE AND OPPOSITE: Line art depicting posters from the True-Life Adventures series of nature films. Produced by Walt Disney from 1948 to 1960, the series includes thirteen groundbreaking documentaries.

ABOVE: Natural environments inspire all manner of storytelling at Pixar Animation Studios, such as with (clockwise from top left) *A Bug's Life* (1998), *WALL·E* (2008), *Up* (2009), and *Finding Dory* (2016).

OPPOSITE: Similarly, flora and fauna influence films at Walt Disney Animation Studios, such as (clockwise from top left) *The Lion King* (1994), *Alice in Wonderland* (1951), *The Jungle Book* (1967), and *Encanto* (2021).

ABOVE: Publishing line art made to represent the savannah featured in *The Lion King* (2019).

OPPOSITE: Publishing line art of the Agrabah Palace from *Aladdin* (2019).

INNOVENTIONS

"In this volatile business of ours . . . we can ill afford to rest on our laurels, even to pause in retrospect. Times and conditions change so rapidly that we must keep our aim constantly focused on the future."

—Walt Disney[T.7]

The concept of "innovation" is nearly synonymous with The Walt Disney Company itself. Beginning with elevating animation from simple cartoons to a true art form—and growing into imagining and engineering the wonders of Walt Disney Imagineering and the latest in film special effects—the design, development, and creative prowess flexed by Disney artists over the decades is a veritable "wizard's workshop." The magic of possibility in *creating* is what entices all dreamers, and the prospects of what tomorrow *can* bring frames up some of the richest and most imaginative projects to have come out of Disney's halls. With a commitment to constant technological experimentation and reinvention, the company inspires and informs new projects in engaging ways.

OPPOSITE: Developmental art by Shane Enoch for the gallery poster from *Disney100: The Exhibition*, 2023.

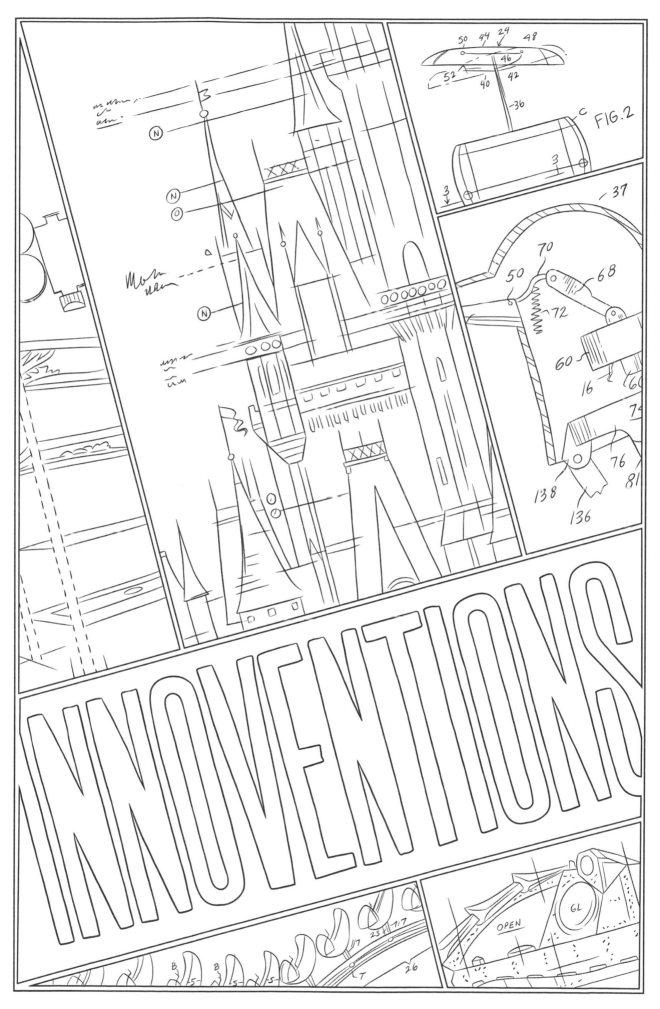

ABOVE: Vintage coloring book line art, *Walt Disney's Disneyville Cut-Out Coloring Book*, 1954.

OPPOSITE: Walt Disney's multiplane camera was a behemoth of innovation that gave an all-new, rich sense of depth to animation. Here we see Walt and his staff with one of the multiplane cameras at the Disney studio in Burbank, California, during the production of *Alice in Wonderland* (1951). Art inked from a photograph by a Disney Studio photographer.

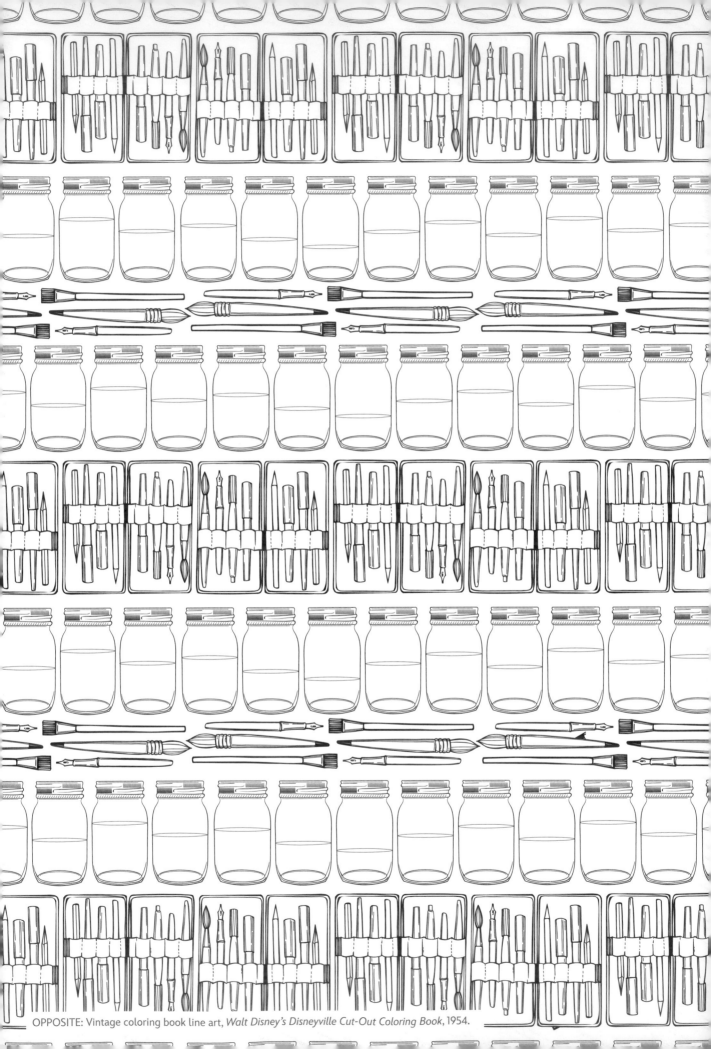

OPPOSITE: Vintage coloring book line art, *Walt Disney's Disneyville Cut-Out Coloring Book*, 1954.

YOUR DISNEY WORLD—A DAY IN THE PARKS

"Disneyland will always be building and growing and adding new things . . . new ways of having fun, of learning things and sharing the many exciting adventures which may be experienced here in the company of family and friends."

—Walt Disney[T.8]

Since 1955, guests have had the chance to step into the many realms of yesterday, tomorrow, fantasy, and adventure as active participants, soaking up Walt Disney's novel idea of a highly curated themed entertainment experience. Now, amounting to some twelve theme parks and dozens of resort hotel sites around the globe, the Disney Parks and Resorts experience is nothing short of a mainstay for international tourism. By providing a forum of entertainment and joy for families and people of all ages to experience and appreciate the cultures and magic of the world around them, Disney Parks and Resorts have provided countless new memories to cherish for those that have visited.

OPPOSITE: Developmental art by Shane Enoch for the gallery poster from *Disney100: The Exhibition*, 2023.

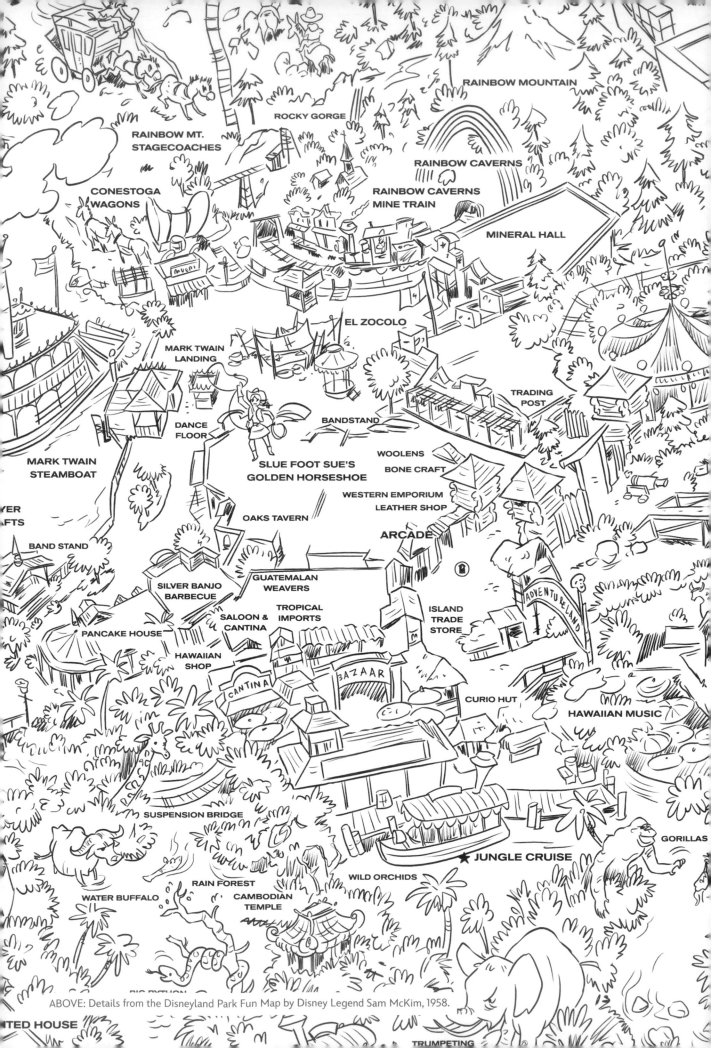

ABOVE: Details from the Disneyland Park Fun Map by Disney Legend Sam McKim, 1958.

ABOVE AND OPPOSITE (clockwise from top left): Matterhorn Bobsleds and the Disneyland Monorail, "it's a small world," Sleeping Beauty Castle, the Haunted Mansion, and *Mark Twain* Riverboat seen through vintage coloring book line art, *A Coloring Book: Walt Disney's Disneyland*, 1983.

ABOVE AND OPPOSITE: Tinker Bell and Dopey on Main Street, U.S.A., vintage coloring book line art, *Walt Disney's Disneyland Coloring Book*, 1956. Background elements from the *Welcome to Disneyland* brochure map, 1958.

ABOVE AND OPPOSITE: Mr. Toad's Wild Ride and Peter Pan's Flight (opposite, bottom), vintage coloring book line art, *Walt Disney's Disneyland Coloring Book*, 1956, and King Arthur Carrousel (opposite, top), vintage coloring book line art, *Walt Disney's Funtime Cut-out Coloring Book*, 1957. Background elements from the *Welcome to Disneyland* brochure map, 1958.

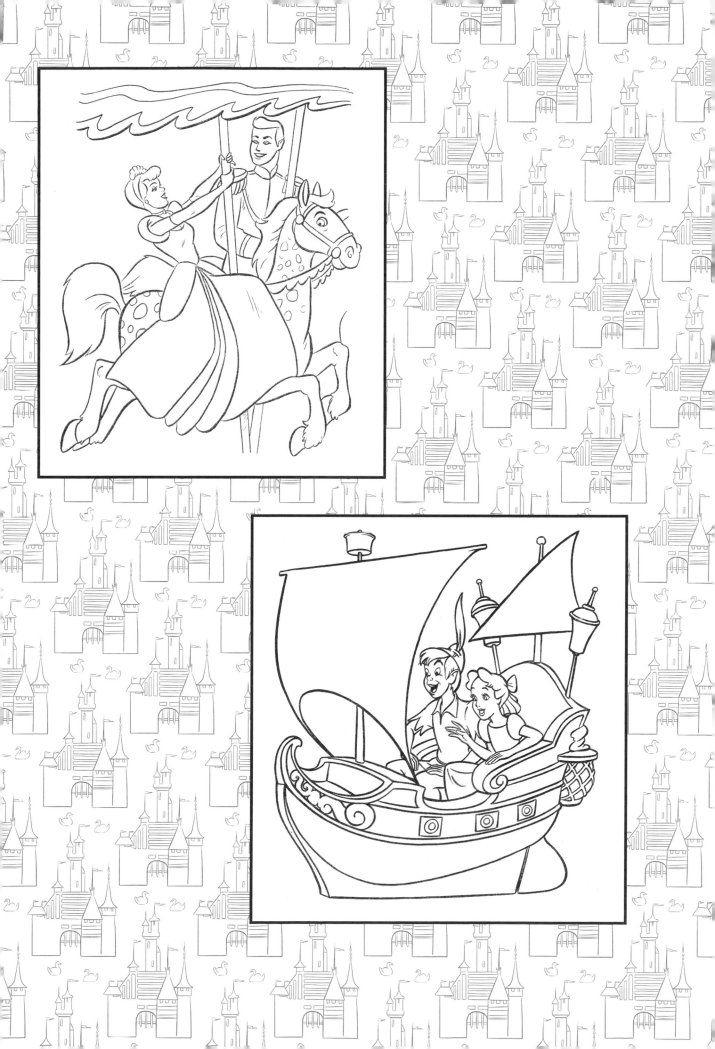

ABOVE: Walt Disney aboard the Jungle Cruise. Art inked from a publicity photograph by a Disney Studio photographer, c. 1959. Background elements from the *Welcome to Disneyland* brochure map, 1958.

OPPOSITE: Big Thunder Mountain Railroad, vintage coloring book line art, *A Giant Coloring Book: Walt Disney's Disneyland*, 1991.

ABOVE: America Sings, vintage coloring book line art, *A Coloring Book: Walt Disney's Disneyland*, 1983. Background elements from the *Welcome to Disneyland* brochure map, 1958.

OPPOSITE: Line art honoring the fan-favorite attraction Space Mountain from the Disney Consumer Products Creative Design team.

THE WONDER OF DISNEY

> "What must concern us more thoughtfully is subject matter. Diversity. We must appeal to a far wider range of audience interest than ever before . . ."
>
> —Walt Disney[T.9]

If there is one factor that has made Disney the global leader in entertainment, it is the emotional connection that exists between the company's beloved characters and their audience. From the moment Mickey Mouse and Minnie Mouse first appeared onscreen in 1928, people couldn't get enough of them. That passionate response led to a demand for ways to bond with Disney characters beyond the big screen. Through all manner of consumer products and later, of course, through television, Disney became a part of our everyday lives. When audiences treasure the experience of seeing a Disney film or show in a theater, catch their favorite streaming series at home, visit a Disney Park in person, or travel the world with their favorite Disney product, they also surround themselves with the wonder, happiness, and joy of what makes Disney special.

OPPOSITE: Developmental art by Shane Enoch for the gallery poster from *Disney100: The Exhibition*, 2023.

ABOVE: The first officially licensed Mickey Mouse product was a children's writing tablet that debuted in 1930.

OPPOSITE: Walt Disney posing with the first large shipment of hand-stitched Mickey Mouse dolls from seamstress Charlotte Clark, 1930 (center). Art inked from a photograph by a Disney Studio photographer. Given the success of the product, Walt and his brother Roy soon licensed the pattern to the McCall company, which allowed eager fans to make Mickey Mouse and Minnie Mouse dolls at home (background).

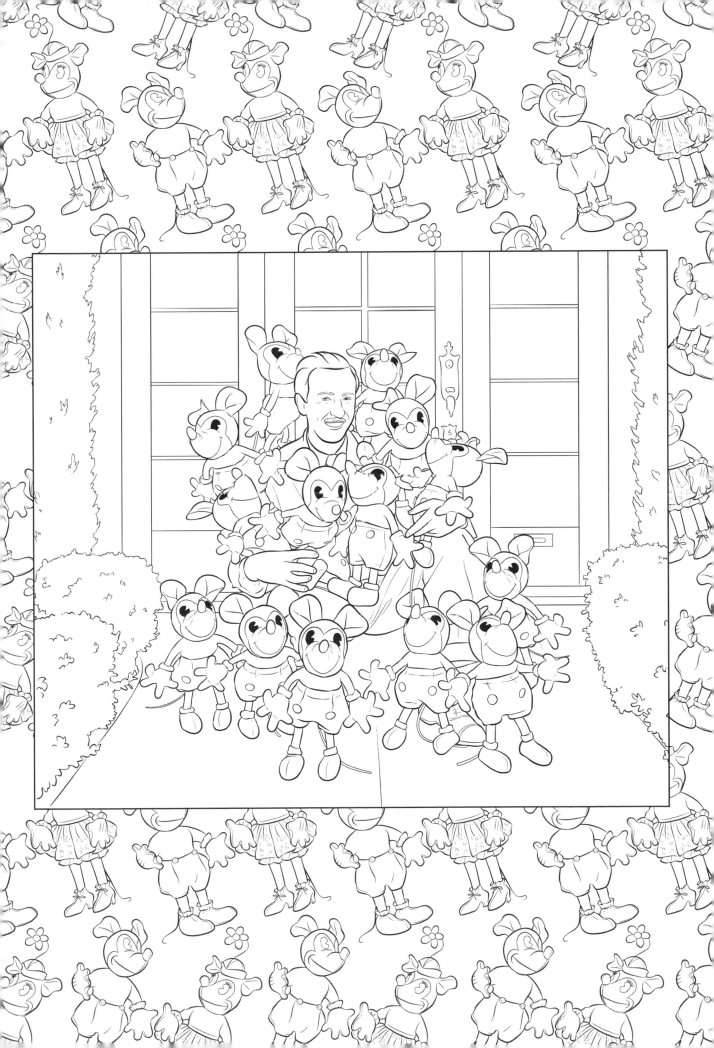

ABOVE AND OPPOSITE: Starting in the 1930s, and running mostly through the 1980s, the company mailed out promotional giveaways called Fan Cards (typically sized around 7¼" × 9" or smaller) to generate interest in upcoming animated features or shorts. The charming cards have since become collector's items. Cards created for (clockwise from top left) *Lady and the Tramp* (1955), *Snow White and the Seven Dwarfs* (1937), *Robin Hood* (1973), *Winnie the Pooh and the Blustery Day* (1968), and *The Aristocats* (1970).

ABOVE AND OPPOSITE: With roots in local theater fan clubs that met with success in the early 1930s, the *Mickey Mouse Club* television series premiered on October 3, 1955, to even greater acclaim.

ABOVE AND OPPOSITE: The 1950s stars of *Mickey Mouse Club*—known as Mouseketeers—first popularized the iconic mouse-ear hat. Today, the fashion trend has evolved and expanded, with fans embracing a variety of mouse-ear headwear. These modern-day illustrations from the Disney Consumer Products Creative Design team celebrate both.

ABOVE: Donald Duck character art, 2022 (background). Vintage coloring book line art, *Walt Disney's Mousekartoon Coloring Book*, 1956. Depicts *The Wise Little Hen* (1934), Donald Duck's first film appearance (top and right).

OPPOSITE: Walt Disney on set during production of the *Disneyland* television series' debut episode, "The Disneyland Story" (1954). Art inked from a photograph by a Disney Studio photographer.

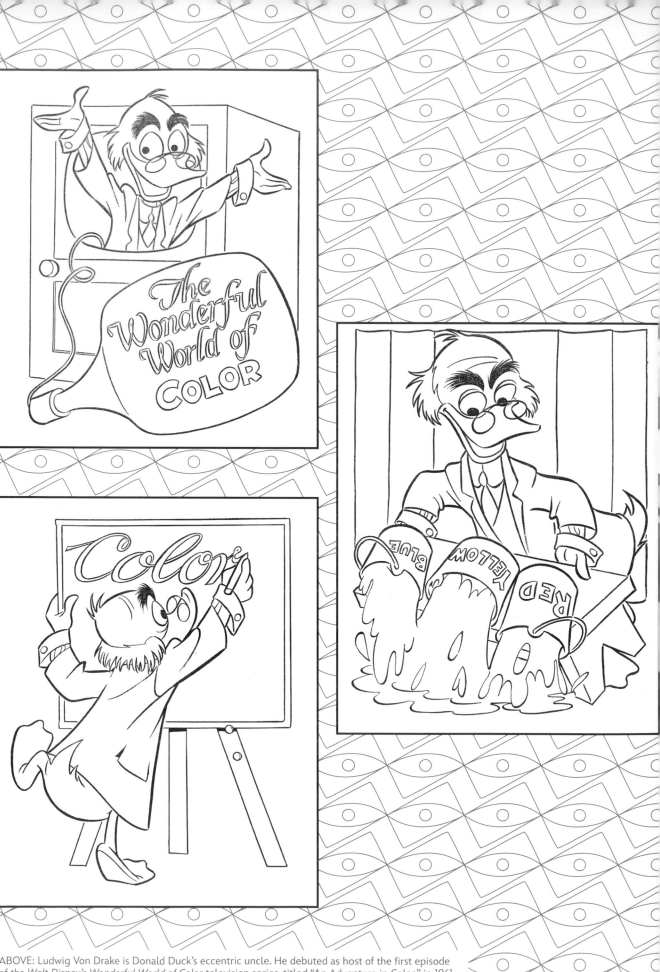

ABOVE: Ludwig Von Drake is Donald Duck's eccentric uncle. He debuted as host of the first episode of the *Walt Disney's Wonderful World of Color* television series, titled "An Adventure in Color," in 1961. Vintage coloring book art, *Walt Disney's Wonderful World of Color*, 1961.

OPPOSITE: The new color title sequence featuring Tinker Bell flying over Sleeping Beauty Castle became a signature moment in the Disney anthology series from 1961 to 1969, and would go on to become nearly synonymous with Disney television programming.

ABOVE AND OPPOSITE: The Disney Afternoon, a two-hour package of animated series, first aired on television on September 10, 1990. Vintage coloring book art (clockwise from top left): *The Adventures of the Gummi Bears Coloring Fun*, 1985; *A Giant Coloring Book: Disney's DuckTales*, 1988; *A Big Color/Activity Book: Disney's Darkwing Duck*, 1991; *A Big Coloring Book: Disney's TaleSpin*, 1990; and *A Big Coloring Book: Disney's Chip 'n Dale Rescue Rangers*, 1989.

WE ARE JUST GETTING STARTED

"I just want to leave you with this thought, that it's just been a sort of dress rehearsal and that we're just getting started. . . ."

—Walt Disney[T.10]

In early 2019, an expansive brainstorm meeting was called across The Walt Disney Company. Employees from all sorts of divisions came together to dream about how we wanted to mark a special milestone occurring on October 16, 2023: Disney's hundredth anniversary. For inspiration, we were given a simple, powerful creed. That mission statement evolved into these thoughts:

It only takes one second of
wonder to inspire a lifetime.
So, imagine what every enchanted
moment from the last 100 years
with Disney has sparked. Bursts of
laugher. Wide-eyed amazement.
Every. Last. Goosebump. . .

So, long live miracle stories
and heart swells, timeless wisdom
and magic spells. And long live the
power of wonder at the heart of
each moment of inspiration.

As we celebrate the first 100
years, may the wonder live on
in all of us for 100 years more.
Long Live Wonder.

OPPOSITE: Developmental art by Shane Enoch and David Pacheco for the gallery poster from *Disney100: The Exhibition*, 2023.

ABOVE: Character sketch art honoring Walt Disney Animation Studios films through the decades, created for the Disney100 Celebration.

OPPOSITE: Disney100 character and icon sketch art commemorating Pixar Animation Studios films.

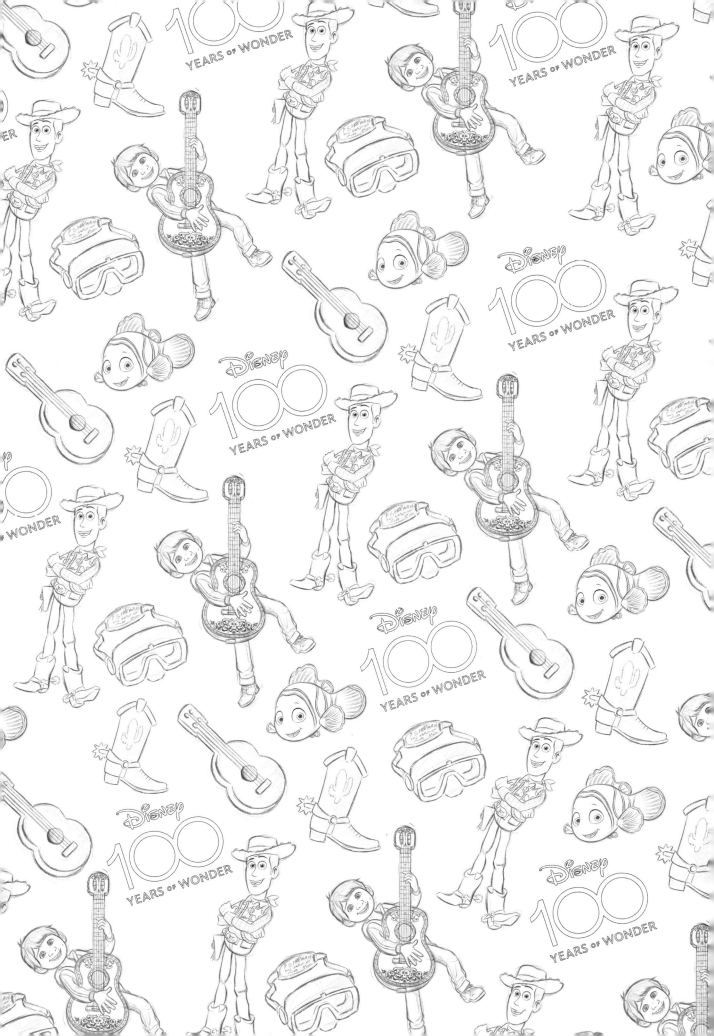

ABOVE: Disney100 art of Minnie Mouse and Mickey Mouse designed for the celebration.

OPPOSITE: Character silhouette art honoring Pixar Animation Studios created for the Disney100 Celebration.

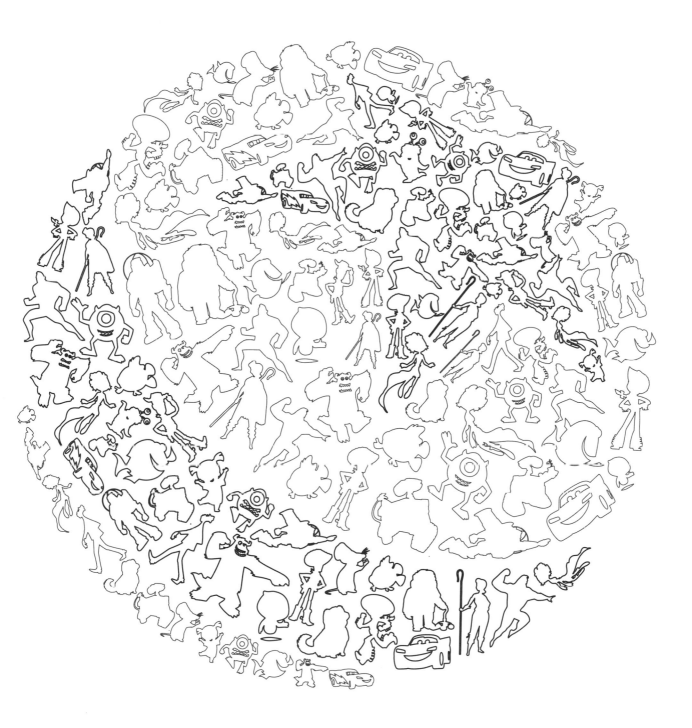

ABOVE: Art Deco–inspired art for the Disney100 Celebration.

OPPOSITE: Design illustration inspired by *Disney100: The Exhibition* main poster by David Pacheco and Shane Enoch, 2023.

ACKNOWLEDGMENTS

No creative enterprise is ever truly the work of one person, and the pages assembled before you are no exception. This book would not have been possible without the generous contributions of the following groups from across The Walt Disney Company:

Pixar Living Archives
Walt Disney Animation Research Library
Walt Disney Archives
Walt Disney Imagineering Art Collection

THIS BOOK'S PRODUCERS WOULD LIKE TO SPECIALLY THANK: Matthew Adams, Justin Arthur, Amy Astley, John Baxter, Holly Brobst, Denise Brown, Michael Buckhoff, Nicole Carroll, Fox Carney, Bob Chapek, Rebecca Cline, Alyce Diamandis, Lynne Drake, the Eastwood family, Shane Enoch, Jeffrey R. Epstein, Maggie Evenson, Darlene Fogg, Christine Freeman, Cesar Gallegos, Erin Glover, Jeff Golden, Howard Green, Don Hahn, Heather Hoffman, Vanessa Hunt, Bob Iger, David Jefferson, Michael Jusko, the Kern family, Alex Koch, Aileen Kutaka, Gary Landrum, Charles Leatherberry, Sarah Luster, Amaris Ma, Ryan March, Daniel Marquand, Matt Moryc, Madlyn Moskowitz, Zenia Mucha, Nikki Nguyen, Tim O'Day, Amy Opoka, Chris Ostrander, Ed Ovalle, David Pacheco, Christina Pappous, Diego Parras, Ty Popko, Joanna Pratt, Chris Rexroad, Juliet Roth, Kristina Schake, Russell Schroeder, Francesca Scrimgeour, Stacy Shoff, Paula Sigman Lowery, SC Exhibitions, Marty Sklar, Dave Smith, Marcy Carriker Smothers, Bruce C. Steele, David Stern, Katie Strobel, Studio TK, Lauren Thomas, the Thomas family, Kimi Thompson, Janice Thomson, Robert Tieman, Melody Vagnini, Steven Vagnini, Julia Vargas, Michael Vargo, Mary Walsh, Cayla Ward, Bob Weis, Anne Wheelock, Alex Williams, Kelsey Williams, Mindy Wilson Fisher.

ALSO, THANK YOU TO THE DISNEY EDITIONS TEAM: Wendy Lefkon, Jennifer Eastwood, Lindsay Broderick, Monica Vasquez, Jerry Gonzalez, and Marybeth Tregarthen.

AND TO THOSE AT DISNEY PUBLISHING: Jennifer Black, Ann Day, Monique Diman-Riley, Michael Freeman, Alison Giordano, Daneen Goodwin, Tyra Harris, Winnie Ho, Jackson Kaplan, Kim Knueppel, Vicki Korlishin, Kaitie Leary, Meredith Lisbin, Warren Meislin, Lia Murphy, Scott Piehl, Tim Retzlaff, Rachel Rivera, Carol Roeder, Zan Schneider, Alexandra Serrano, Fanny Sheffield, Dina Sherman, Ken Shue, Annie Skogsbergh, Megan Speer-Levi, Muriel Tebid, Pat Van Note, Lynn Waggoner, Jessie Ward, and Rudy Zamora.

RIGHT: Vintage publishing cover artwork, *Walt Disney Character Scribble Pad*, mid-1960s.

BIBLIOGRAPHY AND ENDNOTES

T.1, T.2, and T.3 Disney, Walt. *Wisdom*, vol. 32, 1959. (WDA)

T.4 Disney, Walt. Remarks during *Mickey Mouse Club* closed-circuit show, 23 September 1955. (WDA)

T.5 Disney, Walt. *Wisdom*, vol. 32, 1959. (WDA)

T.6 Disney, Walt. *Walt's Files—Byline Stories by Walt Disney*, "Folder 1." (WDA)

T.7 Disney, Walt. Quoted in *Walt Disney Productions Annual Report*, 1950. (WDA)

T.8 Disney, Walt. Quoted in "Welcome to Disneyland," *The Story of Disneyland*, Souvenir Guide Book, 1955. (WDA)

T.9 Disney, Walt. "A Production Viewpoint." *Independent Film Journal*, 01 June 1957. (WDA)

T.10 Disney, Walt. Disneyland Tencennial Awards Presentation, 18 July 1965, Disneyland Hotel, Anaheim, California. Speech. (WDA)

C.1 Sklar, Marty. *Dream It! Do It! My Half-Century of Creating Disney's Magic Kingdoms* (2013, Disney Editions, New York), p. 2.

IMAGE CREDITS

DISNEY100: THE EXHIBTION POSTER ART COURTESY THE WALT DISENY ARCHVIES AND ARTISTS DAVID PACHECO AND SHANE ENOCH on the front and back cover (for ISBN 978-1-368-08370-6) • in the "Where It All Began" chapter, on page 17 • in the "Where Do the Stories Come From?" chapter, on page 29 • in the "The Illusion of Life" chapter, on page 41 • in the "The Spirit of Adventure and Discovery" chapter, on page 51 • in the "The Magic of Sound and Music" chapter, on page 61 • in the "The World Around Us" chapter, on page 71 • in the "Innoventions" chapter, on page 81 • in the "Your Disney World—A Day in the Parks" chapter, on page 87 • in the "The Wonder of Disney" chapter, on page 101 • in the "We Are Just Getting Started" chapter, on pages 117 and 123.

VINTAGE COLORING VIGNETTES FROM PAST PUBLICATIONS: *Mickey Mouse Book*, 1930: in the "Where It All Began" chapter, on page 26 • *Three Little Pigs*, 1933: in the "Where Do the Stories Come From?" chapter, on page 31 • *Donald Duck Color Book*, 1936: in the "Where Do the Stories Come From?" chapter, on pages 32 and 33 • *Walt Disney's Tips on Animation*, late 1950s: in the "The Illusion of Life" chapter, on pages 42 (bottom) and 43 (top right and bottom left) • *How to Draw Chip and Dale: A Walt Disney Character Model Guide*, late 1950s: in the "The Illusion of Life" chapter, on pages 42 (top and center) and 43 (top left, center, and bottom right) • *How to Draw Pluto: A Walt Disney Character Model Guide*, late 1950s: in the "The Illusion of Life" chapter, on pages 44 and 45 • *Walt Disney Productions presents Bedknobs and Broomsticks Coloring Book*, 1971: in the "The Spirit of Adventure and Discovery" chapter, on page 52 (bottom) • Disney studio publicity press book for *Treasure Island* (1950): in the "The Spirit of Adventure and Discovery" chapter, on page 54 • Disney studio publicity press book for *20,000 Leagues Under the Sea* (1954): in the "The Spirit of Adventure and Discovery" chapter, on page 56 (top) • Disney studio publicity press book for *The Island at the Top of the World* (1974): in the "The Spirit of Adventure and Discovery" chapter, on page 56 (bottom) • Disney studio publicity press book for the 1969 theatrical rerelease of *Swiss Family Robinson* (1960): in the "The Spirit of Adventure and Discovery" chapter, on page 58 (top) • *Walt Disney's Fantasia Paint Book*, 1940: in the "The Magic of Sound and Music" chapter, on page 65 • Disney studio publicity press book for *Darby O'Gill and the Little People* (1959): in the "The Magic of Sound and Music" chapter, on page 66 (top) • *Donald Duck Color Book*, 1936: in the "The Magic of Sound and Music" chapter, on page 67 (center, left) • *Walt Disney's Disneyville Cut-Out Coloring Book*, 1954: in the "Innoventions" chapter, on pages 82 and 84 • *Welcome to Disneyland* brochure

map, 1958: backgrounds in the "Your Disney World—A Day in the Parks" chapter, on pages 92–93, 94–95, 96, and 98 • *A Coloring Book: Walt Disney's Disneyland*, 1983: in the "Your Disney World—A Day in the Parks" chapter, on pages 90, 91, and 98 • *Walt Disney's Disneyland Coloring Book*, 1956: in the "Your Disney World—A Day in the Parks" chapter, on pages 92, 93, 94, and 95 (bottom) • *Walt Disney's Funtime Cut-out Coloring Book*, 1957: in the "Your Disney World—A Day in the Parks" chapter, on page 95 (top) • *A Giant Coloring Book: Walt Disney's Disneyland*, 1991: in the "Your Disney World—A Day in the Parks" chapter, on page 97 • *Walt Disney's Mousekartoon Coloring Book*, 1956: in the "The Wonder of Disney" chapter, on page 110 • *Walt Disney's Wonderful World of Color*, 1961: in the "The Wonder of Disney" chapter, on page 112 • *The Adventures of the Gummi Bears Coloring Fun*, 1985, *A Giant Coloring Book: Disney's DuckTales*, 1988, and *A Big Coloring Book: Disney's Chip 'n Dale Rescue Rangers*, 1989: in the "The Wonder of Disney" chapter, on page 114 • *A Big Coloring Book: Disney's TaleSpin*, 1990, and *A Big Color/Activity Book: Disney's Darkwing Duck*, 1991: in the "The Wonder of Disney" chapter, on page 115 • *Walt Disney Character Scribble Pad*, mid 1960s: on "Biography and Endnotes" page 124 • *Walt Disney's Shaggy Dog Coloring Book*, 1959: on "Image Credits" page 126.

PRESENT-DAY COLORING VIGNETTES COURTESY THE DISNEY STORYBOOK ART TEAM in the "Where Do the Stories Come From?" chapter, on pages 38 and 39 • in the "The Spirit of Adventure and Discovery" chapter, on pages 53, 55, 57, 58 (bottom), and 59 • in the "The Magic of Sound and Music" chapter, on page 67 (except for center, left) • in the "The World Around Us" chapter, on pages 76, 77, 78, and 79.

PRESENT-DAY COLORING VIGNETTES COURTESY THE DISNEY CONSUMER PRODUCTS CREATIVE DESIGN TEAM on the front and back cover (for ISBN 978-1-368-09556-3) • on the inside front and back cover and pages 2 and 3 • in the "Contents" section, on page 4 (background) and 5 • in the "Preface" section, on pages 6, 7, 8, 9, 10, 11, 12, 13, 14, and 15 • in the "Where It All Began" chapter, on pages 22, 23, 24, and 25 • in the "Where Do the Stories Come From?" chapter, on pages 31 (background) and 32–33 (background) • in the "The Magic of Sound and Music" chapter, on pages 64–65 (background) and 66 (bottom) • in the "The World Around Us" chapter, on pages 74 (background) • in the "Your Disney World—A Day in the Parks" chapter, backgrounds on pages 90–91, 97, and 99 • in the "The Wonder of Disney" chapter, on pages 106, 107, 108, 109, 110 (background), and 111 (background) • in the "We Are Just Getting Started" chapter, on pages 118, 119, 120, 121, and 122.

SOURCE MATERIALS COURTESY THE ANIMATION RESEARCH LIBRARY AT WALT DISNEY ANIMATION STUDIOS in the "Where Do the Stories Come From?" chapter, on pages 34–35 and 36 • in the "The Illusion of Life" chapter, on pages 46, 47, 48, and 49 • in the "The Magic of Sound and Music" chapter, on pages 62 and 63 (bottom).

SOURCE MATERIALS COURTESY DISNEY THEATRICAL PRODUCTIONS in the "The Magic of Sound and Music" chapter, on pages 68 and 69.

SOURCE MATERIALS COURTESY PIXAR ANIMATION STUDIOS in the "Where Do the Stories Come From?" chapter, on page 37.

SOURCE MATERIALS COURTESY THE WALT DISNEY ARCHIVES AND THE WALT DISENY ARCVHIES PHOTO LIBRARY in the "Contents" section, on page 4 • the "Where It All Began" chapter, on pages 18, 19, 20, 21, and 27 • in the "Where Do the Stories Come From?" chapter, on page 30 • in the "The Spirit of Adventure and Discovery" chapter, on page 52 (top and center) • in the "The Magic of Sound and Music" chapter, on page 63 (top) • in the "The World Around Us" chapter, on pages 72, 73, 74, and 75 • in the "Innoventions" chapter, on page 83 • in the "Your Disney World—A Day in the Parks" chapter, on page 96 (bottom) • in the "The Wonder of Disney" chapter, on pages 102, 103, 104, 105, 111 and 113.

SOURCE MATERIALS COURTESY THE WALT DISNEY IMAGINEERING ART COLLECTION in the "Your Disney World—A Day in the Parks" chapter, on pages 88–89.

ABOVE: Vintage coloring book art, *Walt Disney's Shaggy Dog Coloring Book*, 1959.

OPPOSITE: "There are two ways to look at a blank sheet of paper. . . . It can be the most frightening thing in the world, because you have to make the first mark on it. Or it can be the greatest opportunity in the world, because you get to make the first mark—you can let your imagination fly in any direction, and create whole new worlds!"

—Disney Legend Marty Sklar[C.1]